My Southern Childhood

Pris Campbell

Nixes Mate Books
Allston, Massachusetts

Copyright © 2017 Pris Campbell

Book design by d'Entremont
Cover photo from the collection of Pris Campbell

All rights reserved. This book or any portion thereof may not be reproduced or used in any manner whatsoever without the express written permission of the publisher except for the use of brief quotations in a book review or scholarly journal.

Some of these pieces, in slightly different form, originally appeared in *The Dead Mule School of Southern Literature*.

ISBN 978-0-9991882-2-4

Nixes Mate Books
POBox 1179
Allston, MA 02134
nixesmate.pub/books

For my hometown friends, many of whom are still in my life. You helped make growing up a joyous adventure.

My Southern Childhood

Vignettes of growing up in the late forties and fifties

MY HOMETOWN EMBRACED 2500 souls, one stoplight, one caution light, three churches, two family doctors who came to your house when needed, one beauty shop, two small grocery stores, one motel, a dairy bar, a barbecue place, a dress shop, a hardware store, a dime store, and assorted other family run businesses. Surrounding pine forests, cotton fields, peach arbors, pig farms, and pastures filled with ambling cows and horses, led me to believe it had been set in that exact spot in the rolling Carolina foothills by divine plan to provide us with the best possible place a person could grow up in.

MOTHER TOOK ME with her to Pearl's Beauty Shop, the oldest and first female owned business in our town, in my younger years while she had her hair done. I spent my time drawing while trying to fathom the mysteries of grown-up gossip, comparing the different colors of fingernail polish with my crayons and pretending the roar of the huge dome shaped hair dryers really came from hidden lions, but the machine for giving permanents terrified me with its long cords hanging from the ceiling which attached to heated rods in the victim's head to 'set' the curl. All I could imagine was that one day someone would step out of that chair, hair left in charred bits behind them and decided right then it would never be me.

MOTHER HAD A SPECIAL COLORIZED and framed photograph made of me at age four in Charlotte, common in middle class southern families. My lazy eye was first discovered in that shot. Life with glasses led into my pirate year when my good eye was covered by a patch, causing me to bump into walls or, occasionally, walk off the edge of the side porch into the thick, prickly bushes. Without two good eyes I had no way to know how close a ball was, so was always chosen last for a side in softball games and never made the high school basketball team, though this wasn't explained to me until years later when my view of myself as a sports klutz had already been long embedded into my ego.

BEFORE I KNEW that it was frowned on to go inside a 'colored person's' house even though they came to ours to wash dishes or clean I wandered often down the path to the school janitor's house, property of the school just as our small two-story was. I watched Alma fry fatback and flatbread before we sat on their back porch overlooking the woods, my eyes searching for Indians, unaware until much later of Alma's despair over being told what to do by white people, over knowing she couldn't go downtown on her own, sit in the drugstore and buy a cool soda, or eat in a nice restaurant even if she could afford it, in those separate but equal days we called enlightenment.

MOTHER WOULD SOMETIMES dip my hair in sugar water in my younger years and keep curling it around her finger until I had sausage shaped curls hanging down my back that lasted about long enough for her to snap a photo of me with my doll. When I went to stay with my aunt one summer because Mother was sick, she thought nothing of gussying me up the same way before we took the bus to the park. More gnats must have lived in Columbia than Pageland or else she used too much sugar because they got thicker and thicker around my head until Aunt Orpha said run Priscilla run. Once back in her apartment, the black clotted sugar was washed out, my pigtails revived for the duration.

ON THE CUSP OF WONDERING if Santa was real, my parents, not thinking, stowed the Christmas bag in the back seat with me on our way over to Greenville to my grandparents' apartment where my probing fingers found the outline of a Betsy Wetsy doll, set later under the tree from Santa. I knew then, with an ache inside, that I could never again listen for hooves clattering on the roof top or expect to catch a fat man in red in the parlor munching cookies and checking his list twice, with me singing here comes Santa Claus here comes Santa Claus before the big arrival.

AT VACATION BIBLE SCHOOL we studied the basic catechisms – who God was, that he created the earth, trees, plants and animals and all of us, that he knew every thought we had and nothing was secret from him. Afterwards, we dipped our hands in finger paints smearing bright colors across paper for gifts to take home to our parents, then spilling outside to play games or sit on the church steps, taking special care to not think anything bad that God might overhear.

ON THE SUNDAYS the preacher and his wife came to dinner right after the sermon, Mother paid Alma, to wring one of our chicken's neck. Its headless body raced across our back yard, scaring my cousin Dee into screaming can't make ME eat chicken again, before being dunked in hot water, plucked, cut into its smallest anatomical parts, and fried, in those days when one chicken, plus home-made biscuits, gravy and garden fresh string beans or squash was enough to feed a multitude with no expectations for more.

SOMETIMES WHEN ALMA, who watched out for me while mother taught school, was late meeting me halfway on my quarter mile walk home from kindergarten, Harry, the grown son of Mama Jackson next door, would run out and grab my arms, twirling me over and over until my pigtails came loose. Since Alma couldn't set them right, I had to wait for Mother to come home, hair hanging in knots. I exacted my revenge, however, each night in my bedtime prayers, listing everyone I wanted God to bless and ending with, 'God bless everybody but Harry', despite mother's pleas for forgiveness.

IN EARLY GRADE SCHOOL, before television sets existed in any house I knew of in our town, I tried occasionally to listen to the Lone Ranger on our radio that only worked part of the time, with static interfering with the Lone Ranger's comments to Tonto, his faithful companion, before yelling Hi Ho Silver and rescuing some poor woman or child from evil bandits or lurking Indians. Since radio repair was beyond our budget, not to mention a new radio, I sat with my ear pressed to the speaker on days the reception was good enough, riding the plains along with them until the program was over and I could gather the little boys next door to go explore the woods out back for any lingering bad guys on our own, carrying on the Lone Ranger's work.

SIDEWALK PHOTOGRAPHERS roamed the bigger cites, snapping a photo as you passed, in hopes of selling it to you after. That was how I happened to own a strolling photo of my fourteen year old cousin and my elegant mother, me in-between, grasping their hands in Greenville, still mastering the skill of walking, an ad for a 25 cents club sandwich plastered on a store window behind us where a man wearing fancy pants with pleats in the front, chatted with a man wearing a hat like almost all men wore to town in those days.

DADDY, the district school superintendent, hired Mr and Mrs Hoard to join the grammar school faculty as principal and teacher, then invited them home to meet Mother to make them feel welcome. Deciding that I wanted to entertain them, too, and recently having expanded my knowledge about gender differences by the arrival of a new baby at the house next door I proudly brought a clay doll I had just molded out into the living room, announcing it was a boy, that you could tell by its penis. This exhibition of my talent went very wrong somehow since Mrs Hoard's face turned scarlet and Mother rushed me from the room before I could further discuss the anatomical differences between boys and girls.

RAISED ON A FARM, Daddy believed that a huge breakfast was essential for an energetic day, so he rose long before time for school, despite our complaints over being waked so early, started a big pot of grits, put on his overcoat to slice pieces of ham from the lard coated ham hock twirling in the barn section of the garage, bought yearly at the beginning of our cold season. He then fried eggs, stuck bread into the oven for toast and piggybacked me down the dark cold hall from bedroom to kitchen, carrying me past the kicking donkey lurking in wait, where we sat down to a feast, no longer upset that the sun was still hovering far beneath the horizon.

SHORTLY AFTER MY FOURTH BIRTHDAY, Baylum showed up to eat my mud pies and drink my 'hot chocolate'. He followed me everywhere, so certain he was that I loved him. Mother, appreciating this bond, would hold the door open long enough for him to get inside, and on special occasions would even set him a plate out at supper. She told me later, that many other mothers advised her to stop encouraging me, that my vivid imagination could cause....gasp....MENTAL PROBLEMS when I was older, but mother ignored all of the well-meaning advice, continuing to welcome Baylum into our home until he left of his own accord when I started school.

IN THAT SCIENTIFIC PHASE of my childhood, Carl, my younger neighbor, and I stuck odd shaped rocks into our shorts, bare feet filthy from the sandbox, and played 'I'll show you mine if you show me yours' with the not so bright little girl living nearby since we really wanted to see if she was different from us in that way, too, but when she saw our rocks and cried, my church induced guilt hit. I wondered if she would ever marry after our little adventure, too terrified to see what might one day peek out from her own husband's trousers.

WHILE I WAS STILL SMALL enough to fit on the kitchen counter, Mother lay a towel across it then lifted me up onto my back to wash my hair in the kitchen sink, a method much easier than leaning forward under the bathtub faucet, soapy water streaming into my eyes, or pouring water over my head with a jug in the back yard in warm weather. My cousin Dee Dee stayed with us the summer she was four, screaming until the cows came home when mother tried to wash her hair, prompting Mama Jackson from next door to rush through the back door saying, Camel, is everything okay, is everything okay, but Dee never got used to the hair washing and the screaming went on all summer. Our neighbors, finally convinced this was normal, went about their business as usual and didn't feel compelled to rush to our rescue or call the police.

DURING MY GRAMMAR SCHOOL YEARS, before one burned down and the other closed, our small town supported two theaters where one played cowboy movies on Saturday mornings for a dime for kids, and brought in such celebrities as Zorro who whipped his sword back and forth a few times then signed autographs that I suspected even in my youth didn't match those of other Zorros traveling from town to town. The other theater occasionally played such daring movies as *The Outlaw*, with Jane Russell in her low cut blouse on an outside poster, shocking our mothers into banning us, unsuccessfully, from that end of town.

IF YOU WANTED YOUR HEART BLESSED as a little kid, all you had to do was show a doting aunt or motherly neighbor a recent scrape or cut and they would say bless your heart along with a big hug and a 'Gimme sum sugah' .As I gradually became aware of the other meaning of that blessing, as in bless his heart, he's as dumb as a hill of beans (or a sack of rocks or a tree trunk) it stunned me. A fast learner, I soon learned all the other ways to say insulting things without crossing the line, such as what in tarnation or what in the sam hill are you doing, never knowing who sam hill was or how he got involved in this version of the bad word I wasn't supposed to say. The only exception to that ban being damn yankees, said as if it was all one word, especially in a discussion of Sherman's burning of the South.

THE TUCKERS NEXT DOOR got the first television in our part of town and possibly the whole town, so I would rush next door on Saturday mornings to join Carl and Glenn to sing along with the peanut gallery in Doodyville......WHAT TIME IS IT KIDS.......it's howdy doody time it's howdy doody time. Buffalo Bob talked to the lucky little kids on the show before bringing out Howdy and his puppet friends, then mute, silly Clarabel, who didn't know anything in my opinion about what was funny to kids, and the longed for Princess SummerFall WinterSpring. She always impressed me with her pretty smile and rawhide dresses and left me wondering if more Indians were like her than Tonto or the scalping Indians we read about in school, not knowing until later, of course, that she was no more Indian than I was.

UNDER THE SEAT of our desks in grammar school was a place for us to put the books and papers we weren't using during that particular lesson but the upper lip soon became a place to also store purloined bubble gum before the teacher caught us and unwanted boogers, if one became so bothersome that we couldn't wait until recess to turn our head, dig the darn thing out and flick it oh so casually away into the sand. One boy in our class wasn't at all shy about jamming his finger up his nose and digging them out several times a day in class without trying to hide what he was doing and wiping them off under his desk. I never wanted to pass too close for fear that a dried one would fall loose from the pack onto my foot, causing possible warts or other strange growths to suddenly pop out and deform me in some way.

THE ANNUAL TENT REVIVALS were avoided by the town churchgoers, but my friend Rennie Clare and I, curious, crawled under the shrubs between her house and the tent, watched as the preacher screamed about hell while his salvation seekers shouted 'amen' and 'praise the lord', hoping we might see him hold up a hissing snake or set someone talking in tongues or falling backwards into a trance. Soon, disappointed and bored, we stacked his car seat with dead weeds thinking he might then pull out that snake in divine vengeance, only to have him take his lord's name in vain and stomp through the shrubs, flashlight in hand, in search of us, bellies to ground, shaking.

I WAS ALMOST FIVE when my cousin Dolph returned from war, hit in the head by shrapnel and changed in ways none of us really understood, since 'shell shock' was the only word I heard my aunt and mother use to describe his fits of anger and bad moods. He was so very handsome, walking me down to the corner during Columbia visits for a fountain soda to flirt with the cute, flustered gal behind the counter. I planned to marry him when I grew up, assuming in my young mind that he wouldn't grow older until I caught up with him. Those plans were dashed when he married a woman my aunt referred to as a hussy and the car he was riding in, drunk brother in law at the wheel, crashed, killing him. That crash finished what the war had already tried to do, leaving us all broken hearted for losing him not once but for good the second time.

IN MID-WINTER, when sleet filled the night, writing cobwebbed patterns onto the windows, Daddy rose at four, bundled into his heavy coat and drove the roads checking to see if they were too slick for the school buses to safely navigate. If not, he called his principals, bus drivers, and a core group of teachers who were assigned to call other people armed with lists of names in those pre-internet, no tv days. Soon, phones were ringing all over town, waking slumbering dogs and cats, our own phone ringing nonstop, with eager voices asking 'will there be school today?'. Daddy gave me the important role of saying 'no, stay home' while he warmed his hands before going back out to waylay any stragglers.

MY FIRST REAL EXPERIENCE with the fear of hell when I was seven or so, was when a visiting preacher came to our church and hollered out what sorts of things would send you to that place where your body would burn forever, one reason being if you didn't cleave to your husband or wife and married again. While I didn't understand cleave, I knew that my favorite aunt had been married to a man who had turned mean and hit her and was now married to Uncle Jim, who always made her laugh, so I started crying when we got into the car, prompting Mother to ask what on earth was wrong. When I told her, a devout believer, that I didn't want Aunt Orpha to go to hell, she hushed me and told me Aunt Orpha wasn't going to hell and not to believe a word that fool man said.

MOTHER WAS RAISED PRESBYTERIAN, my father Baptist, so I attended Sunday School and services in her church and some services with my father so I could be versed in both religions to make up my mind which church to join when I came of age. After viewing one baptism at the Baptist Church, the believer completely dunked into a vat of water recessed behind the pulpit, I knew right then that I would choose the Presbyterian Church where they sprinkled the forehead, to avoid the risk of a drowning so early in life.

EVEN MORE THAN HOPSCOTCH, London Bridges, Hide and Seek, Ring Around the Rosie and Jump Rope, my favorite game in grammar school was Red Rover. The real fun was trying to decide who to RED ROVER RIGHT OVER since whoever you held stayed on your team and the ones you couldn't hold got to take someone back with them. What a thrill after the call, all hands locked tight above the wrists with the kid on each side, fierce expressions on our faces, wondering if a linebacker type would spot the fear in your eyes, and choose you and a partner to hit HARD, making that last minute decision to hold on and risk a broken arm or let them plough through.

THE PRESBYTERIAN CHURCH in town and Salem Presbyterian in the country shared the same preacher, so occasionally we shared the same fellowship dinners, tables groaning with fried chicken, okra, cream pies, home-made biscuits and gravy, and casseroles of every kind. The one held at Salem the year before I entered sixth grade was the most memorable, not because the food was set up outside to savor the last bit of summer weather, but because a new boy appeared in front of me suddenly, freckles across his nose, cowlick, and a cast on one arm, his family just moved to town. In that instant, my heart pounding, I abandoned my infatuation with Ronald from first grade on, transferring it to Don in my first experience of discovering how fickle and passing true love could be.

WE SPENT OUR DAYS and evenings over the winter months in our small heated den reading until bedtime or, in later years, watching one program on tv. Until age six, I slept with Mother since her room could be opened to the den allowing enough warm air in to forestall possible colds or flu in one so young. When I grew older, at bedtime Mother would lay my robe over the stove, rush upstairs and spread it across the frigid sheets, calling out come right now. I would dash up after her, slippers flopping, and dive onto the rapidly cooling robe just as she pulled four army blankets up over me, teeth chattering until my shivering body finally heated the cocoon of covers and I slept.

MOTHER, LIKE MANY SOUTHERNERS I knew, was a great weaver of stories, both with her first graders and when relatives gathered over the holidays. Her two most requested encores were always the one about when her cousin Sudie cheated on the bible exam, which elicited our tears of laughter, and the one that brought tears of sadness, when mother's papa told her five year old brother that their mother, taken down by the great flu epidemic of 1919, had gone to live with God, whereupon Uncle Herman said 'but doesn't God know a little boy needs his mama'?

THE FEED AND SEED was one of the two places you could buy groceries and where farmers could also pick up their seed and other farming needs. A bonus for teachers was that over the summer when no salary was coming in, the store would let you sign your grocery bill and hold it, trusting completely that you would pay as soon as you could. What I remember most is that when we needed a few things badly and Daddy was using the car, if we called with a list, Buzz would show up with our groceries in the back of his pickup, having shopped for us and delivered at no extra charge, like he did for anyone who called, a kindness that touched me even as a kid.

WE KNELT TREMBLING, hands over our heads beside our desks at school drill time in those days our parents referred to as the Cold War, believing we would be sheltered from crashing glass if Russia bombed us. Some grown-ups even built bomb shelters stocked with food, jugs of water, purifying tablets, and gas masks. Still young and innocent, my classmates and I were unaware that a bomb would change our life as we knew it, trusting that Ike and our parents would carry us safely through all the frightening places to that as yet unknown place called adulthood.

APPOINTED BY THE OTHER MOTHERS as reluctant chaperone to Ella Ruth, Kay and me for our first group rock and roll show at the Charlotte Coliseum where Chuck Berry did his famous strut, Jerry Lee screaming Great Balls of Fire, feet and rump pounding the piano keys at one point, bleached hair waving, followed by Clyde McPhatter's smooth croon, the mostly 16 or under audience screaming, some making out between songs. Mother sat with her hands folded, a calm expression on her face, never once complaining about this teens-gone-crazy world she'd been thrown into.

MY BEST FRIEND IN NINTH GRADE folded her love notes, written on lined notebook paper, four time over lengthwise than up from the bottom to the size of a small matchbook, tucking in the ends the way she'd seen older girls do it. When her wannabe Romeo-turned-Judas found a girl he could have his way with under the community center, a popular deflowering place built high on concrete pillars with thick bushes and trees all around for privacy, he drove through town tossing my friend's love notes out his window for the town fathers and mothers to read or be washed down into the gutters to be lost forever with the next rain.

ON DADDY'S FIRST TRIP AWAY from the Carolinas or Georgia in his life, he flew to Seattle to attend an educator's conference where dinner was served in the famous Space Needle, so wanting to ensure that he got regular milk and not buttermilk from the waitress, possibly unaware of southern dietary idiocentricities, he was careful to ask for 'sweet' milk, eliciting a puzzled look, then, 'umm.....we don't have sweet milk but I can bring you a glass of milk and a bowl of sugar'.

THE COOL BOYS with ducktails and pegged pants who could afford a used, fixed-up car, competed in who could put the fanciest spinners on their hubcaps before drag racing on one of the many country roads encircling our town. This gave my friend Ella Ruth and me the clever idea of putting rocks in the cute new teacher from Charleston's hubcaps. We laughed at how he would think something horrible was happening to his car, but, instead, he calmly stopped, removed the rocks and went on his way so casually we were certain he must have spotted us 'doing the evil deed'.

BEFORE THE BYPASS around town was built, we sat in Kohler's drugstore drinking cherry coke and listening to the juke play the top hits, when the summer yankees stopped in on their way to Myrtle Beach for a cool drink or snacks. Seeing the women dressed in baggy bermuda shorts and clip-on sunglasses flipped up under wide visors over frumpy hair, caused us to wonder if women from Sherman's homeland were taught any sense of style as we southerners had been almost from birth.

SHA NA NA SHA NA NA NA NA, sha na na na na sha na na na, sha na na na na Yip yip yip yip yip yip yip yip mum mum mum mum mum mum get a job…blaring out of Judy's father's pickup truck, one of the few vehicles in town with a radio, loaned occasionally, as parents did, after we got our driver's license at 14. We sang along, knowing every sha and nip, every get a job line in this song our mothers rolled their eyes over but the crazy, poetic, nonsensical music took root as we cruised the streets of our town, embedding every house, every street, every person, every teen love into the cells of our body to emerge again whenever the old songs played.

IN THE COLDER MONTHS when it was impossible to use the hand wringer washing machine on the screened back porch, Mother washed anything washable in the bathroom sink, next to the warm den. At least once a week, a maze of wooden hanging racks was filled with underwear, stockings, nightgowns and pajamas until their moisture formed ice on the den windowpanes and we struggled to squeeze in and out of the small room. My crinolines, the sole exception to this laundry strategy, twirled in wide starched circles on the frigid clothes line behind the garage like alien spacecraft.

ALL OF THE HOMES I knew in those early days were stocked with meal supplies but never with chips, cookies or sodas, so once I had my allowance of 25 cents a day, beginning in eighth grade, I bought bottled cokes dripping with freezing cold water for a dime at Joyner's or cherry cokes at Kohler's drugstore, saving up for a weekly chicken salad sandwich made by Mrs Kohler, a banana split at the Dairy Bar, our Saturday night hangout to meet out of town boys, a barbecue sandwich at Presses or an occasional trip to the Monroe drive in theater, which cost a whopping two day allowance, prompting some of us to hide in the trunk. When I achieved the ability to deep fry my own doughnuts, one of my first successful ventures into cooking, my friends and I ate until our bellies were packed, thrilled by the possibilities of that day's freed-up allowance.

OUR ELVIS PRESLEY FAN CLUB, consisting of eight members, met at Judy's house. Membership was earned by giving the correct answers to such questions as what was his middle name, where was he born, and would we promise him our lasting loyalty. Satisfied that we were a true blue club we enlisted two boys we knew to help build our Elvis clubhouse and when we heard one fan had let Elvis sign his name just at the dip of her scooped blouse I promised myself secretly that if I ever met him I would also get his autograph, but in indelible ink, just at the top of my own trembling triple A's to keep it close to my heart, beating in time to Love Me Tender.

DURING PRAYER MEETING every Wednesday night, we gathered to sing the gospel hymns deemed too undignified for Sundays, bookended by a long preacher prayer at start and finish, and punctuated by the swish of paper fans decorated with a pale, brown haired Jesus in a white robe, provided by the local funeral home during the hot summer months when air conditioning was a luxury not yet found in our town.

TWICE A YEAR, several of my classmates and I met at my house or Kathy's for our spend-the-night parties, the only two houses that could accommodate five or six giggling girls far enough away from our parents to allow their sleep, gabbing about which boy was cutest, who had a crush on who, or juicy town gossip. We then struck poses for posterity for my brownie, mops on our heads, Pepsi's thrust forward, and, once, my father's rubber boots on my feet. The last shot inevitably showed our eyes barely open, hair rumpled, dawn streaming into the room, no longer prepared to repeat our performance art from the night before.

WHILE OTHER PLACES sometimes claimed they were the Watermelon Capitol of the World, we knew we truly had achieved that honor because every July Miss America came to our town, along with other beauty queens vying for Watermelon Queen in their colorful gowns and bathing suits, while truckloads of ripe, yummy watermelons, barefoot police girls fining men who came to town wearing shoes and women without aprons cemented our reputation. TV cameras were trucked down from Charlotte, to record seed spitting and watermelon eating contests, topped off by a parade through town, the shriners circling, bands blaring, girls on the backs of convertibles tossing smiles as sweet as our iced tea to those of us cramming ourselves forward for a last look at summer peaking before us.

I FELL IN LOVE WITH PAUL NEWMAN at the Monroe Drive-in the second those blue eyes looked down at me from the screen in *The Long Hot Summer*, instantly tying him with Elvis in my most ardent affections. I pretended he would walk off the screen, pull me into the backseat for a long, lingering kiss, transforming me into one of those fallen women my friends and I read about in the forbidden romance magazines we hid inside of movie magazines at Thomas' Drug Store or in *Lady Chatterley's Lover*, passed among us until mother finally found it hidden under my mattress, fortunately after I had read the best parts.

OUR BELOVED FAMILY DOCTOR who had brought me through measles and other mishaps of youth was the only prominent citizen in town who didn't attend church, didn't believe Jesus saved us or in baptism or the existence of the devil, even though his wife was a devoted member of the Presbyterian church, so representatives of the town fathers arrived at the back door of his office one day to convince him he would go to hell if he didn't change his beliefs. Tolerant of this mission to rescue him from the devil's door for only so long, he chased them all out with a few choice words warning them never to return unless they needed a broken arm fixed or caught the flu and were at death's door.

AS TV STARTED SHOWING us more of the world we first saw yankees pour red sauce over chicken, grilling it, then calling it barbecue. We were stunned since everybody knew that real barbecue involved cooking a pig for hours in a pit over hickory, rubbing a secret vinegar-based sauce into the meat until it was so tender you could pull it apart, then mounding it onto a bun with cole slaw on top. The only places I knew of in our town where you could get this this properly prepared were at Presses Grill or at the annual Lions Club barbecue where the pigs started cooking while it was still dark, my father in charge of preparing the sauce the day before, this feast drawing most of the town, clad in our best summer clothes, paper plates bent with food.

IN OUR SMALL TOWN, doors were never locked except at night or when going to see an out of town relative, so good friends and neighbors came to the back door into the hall and kitchen, walking on in after a rap and a hollered hello, while slightly more formal visitors knocked on the side door into the living room, but waited for someone to come. Only strangers knocked on the front door, one that stayed locked simply since it was stuck so hard that only Daddy could open it, leaving Mother or me, when home alone, to shout through the thick wood 'go around to the side', sometimes successfully, other times fruitlessly until the person drove off before we could rush outside to find out if the matter was urgent.

AT FOURTEEN OR SO, most of my friends and I entered that next step towards adulthood by being allowed on special occasions such as church or a chaperoned dance to wear low versions of pointy toe spike heels with stockings, hooked to a complicated garter belt with dangling straps for attaching hose with seams down the back that never seemed to stay straight. This stage of growing up was an acquired skill, we discovered, so we wobbled about at first like we were drunk, twisting our ankles, getting stuck in cracks in the pavement, occasionally dragging strands of toilet paper, and envying the smooth, assured stride of the older, more proficient girls.

LIVING IN A STATE where liquor couldn't be served at a restaurant or bar and where a liquor store couldn't label itself as such by a sign, didn't mean the people who wanted to drink couldn't find it to drink at home. It was common knowledge that buildings painted white on the side with a large red dot in the center, known as the Red Dot stores, were the place to go, preferably one a ways out of town where brown bags could be hidden under a jacket, with a quick getaway down the road, before someone you knew spotted you and spread the news throughout town unless everybody knew you were a drunk and not worth further comment.

MOTHER'S SEWING WAS LIMITED to taking up an occasional hem or sewing on missing buttons so we made our annual trek to Belks in Charlotte each August to buy our clothes for the year. The only exceptions allowed to the 'no new clothes in-between' rule were a couple of pairs of summer shorts and a colorful dress for Easter with our choice of various skull hugging hats, hats that looked like upside down boxes with veils, brimmed hats open on top, or, one outrageous year, a bright green hat that made me look like I was balancing a saucer on my head on my way to celebrate our risen Lord.

GROWING UP, nobody ever told me I was expected to pronounce the 'g' in 'ing' words. We all knew that MAAgret and PEEcan were the right way to say those particular words. Nobody treated you like you were stupid if you said I'm fixin' to do that, it's on down the road a piece or I usetacould do that, and you knew that y'all ALWAYS referred to more than one person even if asking only your best friend 'what are y'all having for supper tonight'. Most of all, for girls and women, at least, your father was always Daddy or Papa even if you were turning eighty, so when television sets became fairly common in late grammar school we were constantly surprised at how people from up north so casually slayed the English language.

DADDY KEPT A VEGETABLE GARDEN out behind our house for as long as I can remember, having worked out ways to make our naturally sandy or red clay soil richer by ploughing cow manure into the fall earth from nearby farms, recruiting me occasionally to help him shovel it into a large container, rotating the crops each year so the soil didn't get worn out. My mother's summers away from teaching were spent snapping beans, cutting up squash, husking and scraping corn cobs, peeling cucumbers for pickling and stewing tomatoes, getting them ready for the tedious job of canning so we could have vegetables lined up in the cupboards to keep summer with us throughout the long cool winter.

OUR EIGHTH GRADE CLASS had our big dance at the community center in the woods next to Pearl Arant's house, where we we took care choosing top 45's such as Tutti Frutti, Maybeline or Only You, to get everyone dancing. Most of the boys either didn't want to jitterbug, though, or hadn't learned how yet, a skill we girls felt was important, like kissing the back of your hand to be ready for the real thing or stuffing your bra with tissues to look your best at boy girl events. Finally we gave up trying to cajole the boys into trying and jitterbugged with each other, hand to hand, bobby socks swishing back and forth around the floor.

I NEVER COULD FIGURE OUT WHY zits always appeared exactly when you wanted to look your best or why they always popped out right where a person would have to be blind not to notice, not to mention that despite all the ads about Clearasil covering them up and drying them out, when you put it on, it mostly looked like you had a brown spot on your face and it never really dried them up to get rid of them. Whenever one popped out on my face, big enough to be mistaken for the beginning of measles I tried all sorts of casual poses that involved putting my hand to my face to cover the offending blotch, jealous of those girls whose smooth, spotless faces looked as clear as the ads said mine would be if I used it, but never was.

THE BAND AND CHEERLEADERS were transported in a big yellow school bus to out-of-town football games where the cheerleaders waved pom poms and yelled Go Tigers Go into the crisp autumn air until halftime when the band marched, horns blaring and clarinets squawking. Pleased with ourselves, we piled back into the bus after the game, moving from seat to seat before settling down to sing all the Do Wap songs – In The Still of The Night and Come Go With Me always our favorites, until, exhausted, we finally fell quiet and let the bus rumble us on home through the dark, southern night.

ONCE A MONTH, our small school newspaper, in addition to publishing the football and marching band schedule , featured one of my favorites, the Jiggs and Judy gossip column, where we learned such things as a certain boy in the eleventh grade with the initials 'CC' had been eying a girl with short, dark hair in the sophomore class lately or that 'DG' might be asking his honey to go steady soon if those big smiles on his face meant anything. In an early issue, the eighth graders entering high school were rated as best of something and I was chosen best mouth. I wasn't sure if my mouth was pretty or if this meant I talked too much since it surely hadn't been picked out for best kissing yet by any boy.

OUR HOME PHONE was on a party line with my father's office. Since his business was often private and if I was on the home phone he would get on his line and say 'hang up Priscilla', ending my conversation right then. But my good friend shared a line with the town gossip. One of our sources of much merriment was waiting for her to quietly....she thought... come on to listen so we could start talking about outlandish things that had never happened just to see how fast they were spread through town.

AS WE GREW OLDER, those of us with straight as stick hair wished we had nice waves that would comb out each morning and make our bangs fluff and hair turn up in a flip if we tired of ponytails, trying to make it stay wound under bobby pins, which made us miserable no matter which way we turned, hoping some of them didn't come loose in the night, especially when our hair was so slippery after we washed it. We envied boys who never had to go through this with their crewcuts and ducktails since they could just get up, comb their hair with Butchwax or Brylcream, creating elaborate ducktails that could be undone and redone without the torture of a bobby pinned night.

BY HIGH SCHOOL, any girl HAD to have a wallet with a lot of cellophane picture holders filled, first of all, with your boyfriend, if you had one, with maybe a lipstick kiss on the picture, then whatever photos you could get of your friends or a group of friends hanging out somewhere together. Once the photos were in the wallet, sides bent to make them fit when necessary, little sayings were printed by hand or clipped from a magazine, such as GOOD TIMES or BEST FRIENDS, but sometimes just the names, all tucked down towards the bottom of the picture pocket to be passed around when we got together, always being certain to check when you got your wallet back since slipping a favorite photo out was to sometimes be expected.

AT SIXTEEN it seemed suddenly that sweet sixteen and never been kissed was on everyone's lips and nearly every girl I knew had already been kissed, some as early as thirteen. Only one boy had ever asked when we were hanging out, riding the country roads around our town one day, a common alternative to hanging out at the drugstore, I'd turned him down because you were expected to go on a real date first, preferably two or risk being called loose, but boys could kiss all they wanted with as many girls as would kiss them back and never be judged or gossiped about.

NEAR THE END OF MY JUNIOR YEAR in high school I was invited to attend an early admissions summer program at Stetson University and I went to get a feel for being taught by college professors, not for the purpose of skipping my senior year. I departed to harder, exciting classes and discovered the exhilaration of no longer being labeled 'the superintendent's daughter', viewed with discomfort by some teachers all through school, concerned I would report on their teaching, even though I never mentioned them, good or bad. I begged my parents to let me go, to empty their nest early, unbind my wings, until they painfully agreed. I gave up being senior newspaper editor, last drugstore hangouts, the prom, that proud march down the aisle to Pomp and Circumstance, fried green tomatoes on chilly nights, scuppernongs straight off the vine, my dear friends and parents, and headed out into a new world, one foot left behind always in my beloved home and hometown.

About the Author

The free verse poetry of Pris Campbell has appeared in numerous journals, such as *PoetsArtists. Rusty Truck, Bicycle Review, Boxcar Poetry Review*, and *Outlaw Poetry Network*. Her last book, *Squall Line on the Horizon*, a book of romantic tanka, was published by Nixes Mate Books. Her haiku, tanka and haiga publications include *Frogpond, cattails, Acorn, Haigaonline, One Hundred Gourds*, and *Failed Haiku*. The Small Press has published six collections of her free verse poetry and Clemson University Press a seventh one, a collaboration. A former Clinical Psychologist, sailor and bicyclist until sidelined by ME/CFS in 1990, she makes her home in the Greater West Palm Beach, Florida.

Nixes Mate Books features small-batch artisanal literature, created by writers that use all 26 letters of the alphabet and then some, honing their craft the time-honored way: one line at a time.

More Nixes Mate titles:
ON BROAD SOUND | Rusty Barnes
KINKY KEEPS THE HOUSE CLEAN | Mari Deweese
SQUALL LINE ON THE HORIZON | Pris Campbell
COMES TO THIS | Jeff Weddle
HITCHHIKING BEATITUDES | Michael McInnis
AIR & OTHER STORIES | Lauren Leja
WAITING FOR AN ANSWER | Heather Sullivan
A WORLD WHERE | Paul Brookes

Forthcoming titles from Nixes Mate:
NIXES MATE REVIEW ANTHOLOGY 2016/17
CAPP ROAD | Matt Borczon
LUBBOCK ELECTRIC | Anne Elezabeth Pluto
SECRET HISTORIES | Michael McInnis

nixesmate.pub/books

www.ingramcontent.com/pod-product-compliance
Lightning Source LLC
Chambersburg PA
CBHW052135010526
44113CB00036B/2265